Elaine Rodrigues Nichio
Maria Helena Ferrari
Adriana Willers

The classroom: a space for humanisation and reader training

Elaine Rodrigues Nichio
Maria Helena Ferrari
Adriana Willers

The classroom: a space for humanisation and reader training

Reflections and teaching practices

ScienciaScripts

Imprint

Any brand names and product names mentioned in this book are subject to trademark, brand or patent protection and are trademarks or registered trademarks of their respective holders. The use of brand names, product names, common names, trade names, product descriptions etc. even without a particular marking in this work is in no way to be construed to mean that such names may be regarded as unrestricted in respect of trademark and brand protection legislation and could thus be used by anyone.

Cover image: www.ingimage.com

This book is a translation from the original published under ISBN 978-3-330-76706-5.

Publisher:
Sciencia Scripts
is a trademark of
Dodo Books Indian Ocean Ltd. and OmniScriptum S.R.L publishing group

120 High Road, East Finchley, London, N2 9ED, United Kingdom
Str. Armeneasca 28/1, office 1, Chisinau MD-2012, Republic of Moldova, Europe
Printed at: see last page
ISBN: 978-620-8-11230-1

Thanks

I dedicate this work mainly to my children, Ana Isabela and Luiz Augusto, for all my absences.

I thank God for the privilege of achieving my goals.

To my parents, Augusto and Luzenir, for teaching me values that are essential to the formation of my character.

To my husband, Anderson, for his support and affection.

Thank you to my colleagues in my professional career, as they have all been instrumental in bringing together the experiences that have now come to fruition through this book.

Presentation

It is with great joy that I publish in this book reflections on reading in the classroom, together with some suggestions for working with the literary object. The results of the discussions are based on professional experience combined with academic theories. However, the book goes beyond a simple theoretical approach, as it is based on its applicability in everyday school life, i.e. inside the classroom.

The chapters in this book present work developed in the school context, which in turn has been tested and proven, in order to measure its effectiveness and achieve the proposed objectives.

Present in the work is Adriana Willers, a Portuguese language teacher with whom we have developed several projects together at the Isolina Ruttmann-Sesi/Vilhena-Social Service of Industry Educational Center. Maria Helena Ferrari, a researcher and English language teacher at the Federal Institute of Rondonia, has also worked with us on interdisciplinary projects.

These approaches are the result of work carried out by the "Languages, Arts and Humanities in Contemporary Education -

LINAHC" research group. They are arranged in three chapters that integrate theory and teaching practice. In this way, the book provides an opportunity to rethink the role of the school in forming citizens/readers, as well as the role of the teacher and the family in this very important process. Finally, it presents proposals for projects that encourage the practice of reading and consequently help to build up the humanizing aspect of the reader.

I hope that both the reflections on reading and the suggestions for projects can guide the work done in the classroom by teachers of both Portuguese and other subjects, because the importance of reading does not depend on the subject, as it is essential for the formation of citizens who participate in society.

Elaine Rodrigues Nichio

SUMMARY

CHAPTER I

1. THE IMPORTANCE OF READING

Reading has been a human need since the dawn of time, since man needs to be situated in time and space. Knowing what is going on around him is indispensable for ensuring his own survival. More than that, reading is an important vehicle for the creation, transmission and transformation of culture. According to Coelho:

> (...) the impulse to "read", to observe and understand the space in which one lives and the beings and things with which one lives, is a basic human condition. Ever since human intelligence was able to organize the forms and situations faced by humans in their daily lives into a coherent whole, they have been driven to record those fleeting experiences in something durable. The discovery of cave art from 12 or 15 thousand years ago by archaeologists shows unequivocally this essential impulse that led man to express his life experiences in a form (realistic or allegorical). (2000, p.16)

In this way, we can see that reading is a human achievement, in which all of society, in its different evolutionary stages, produces cultural baggage, thus becoming an instrument for knowledge and transformation of the entire culture of an era. However, each individual has a particular type of reading, the reading of the world, which is closely linked to culture and is not necessarily learned at school. Freire says of reading the world:

> The reading of the world precedes the reading of the word, so that the subsequent reading of the word cannot be without the continuity of the reading of the word. Language and reality are dynamically linked. The understanding of the text to be achieved by its critical reading implies the perception of the relationship between the text and the context.

It can be seen that there is reading of the world and reading of the word, in which the act of reading goes beyond the simple decoding of words, because reading of the world involves dimensions that precede the discovery of reading through literacy, involving the way in which each individual positions themselves in relation to what is around them. Thus, the two types of reading complement each other, resulting in critical and democratic reading.

Reading is a possibility for reflection and re-creation. It is the path that opens up man's existence so that he can form new meanings. Learning to read involves prior learning, which means reading the world and its contexts, and for Freire (1998, p.29) these are learnings that interact: "From the outset, in democratic and critical practice, reading the world and reading the word are dynamically combined".

The act of reading is one of the main ways in which human beings question themselves as subjects and objects, as it paves the way for their awareness. Each reader comes into existence and gains their own individuality as they unveil and experience the meanings mediated by their world.

This is a complex process that broadens and integrates knowledge and intellect. In this context, Coelho states that:

> The act of reading stimulates the exercise of the mind; the perception of reality in its multiple meanings; the awareness of the self in relation to the other; the reading of the world on its various levels, and above all, stimulates the study and knowledge of the language of meaningful and conscious verbal expression. (2000, p.16)

You have to read very carefully as you enter the world that the text offers, because reading is not just about memorizing and marking up a text. The act of reading involves the reader's critical opinion, interpretation and rewriting of what has already been read and understood, making it possible to acquire different points of view and broaden experiences.

One of the main effects of reading is the improvement of language, of expression, both individually and collectively, because a society that knows how to express itself, knows how to say what it wants, is less manipulated.

1.1. Reading at school

According to Mello (1995, p.169) "for the majority of children
In Brazil, school is effectively the only place where people come into contact with books and reading situations". It is clear that the school is the privileged space for the formation of the reading habit, because given the absence of books and reading situations in the family, the stimulation of reading depends on the quality of the work carried out by the school.

Recognizing the importance of the school in forming the habit of reading, it is necessary to reflect on the reading practice developed in the school environment.

For Kaufman (1995, p13) "Texts, as units communicative texts manifest different intentions on the part of the sender: they seek to inform, convince, seduce, entertain and suggest moods". In this way, the texts are presented in a different way, meeting the preferences of each reader and increasing the number of assiduous readers, so the texts must be articulated in such a way as to interest the students.

It is clear that reading at school must be a teaching tool, and that in order for it to become an object of learning, it must make sense to the student. The Portuguese Language Curriculum Parameters (1998, p.55) provide a selection of reading procedures to be adapted to the different objectives and interests of the subject (study, personal training, entertainment, task accomplishment) and the characteristics of the genre and medium:

- **Integral reading:** reading a text sequentially and extensively;

- **Inspectional reading:** using procedures to choose texts for further reading;

- **Topical reading:** identifying specific information in the text, locating entries in a dictionary or encyclopedia;

- **Proofreading:** identifying and correcting, in a given text, certain inadequacies in relation to an established standard;

- **Reading item by item**: carrying out a task following commands that presuppose a necessary order.

Therefore, the school must prepare students to understand what they read, making them capable of going beyond the meanings of words, contextualizing the text, anticipating it, being able to relate what they read to previous readings, validating their reading by locating stylistic and discursive elements.

According to Rangel (1990), reading is a basic practice, essential for learning. Nothing replaces reading, even in an age of proliferating audiovisual and computer resources. Reading is an essential part of work, commitment, perseverance and dedication to learning. The habit of reading comes from practice and is not always a pleasurable act, but it is always necessary. For this reason, stimuli must be used to introduce students to the habit of reading.

It is the school's responsibility to provide its students with the conditions to access knowledge. In this cycle of creating and recreating knowledge, which is typical of school life, reading undoubtedly occupies a very important place. And so we have the teacher as a relevant subject in this process, and below are some considerations about the role of the educator in the school environment.

1.2. The role of the teacher

Noting the presence of reading in schools is relatively easy, but it is a little more difficult to discuss the concrete conditions of reading production. The relevance and necessity of reading for teachers and students are irrefutable, but it is necessary to critically analyze the existing conditions and the ways in which this act is conducted in the school context.

The authoritarian ways in which textbooks are presented in the classroom tend to contribute to student rejection, according to Sandroni and Machado:

> The book should be presented and experienced by the pupil without any kind of imposition, but as a source of pleasure, stimulating curiosity and interest in the world [...] For the proposals to be successful, the teacher responsible is expected to have effective availability, a taste for reading and good linguistic information. It's obvious to say that you can only teach what you know. (1987, p.60)

When teachers arouse their students' interest in reading, the activity becomes pleasurable and voluntary, gradually encouraging them to read different genres and increasing their potential as readers.

However, developing the habit of reading in students is a task that must be carried out gradually. Bamberger states that:

> Teachers who give their pupils "small doses" of the importance of reading every day - in their encounters with reading, as support for their school work and for their personal interests in all school subjects, teachers who try to make these small "habit doses" effective in daily leisure activities and as homework, teachers who do this systematically throughout the child's school career, without forcing, but naturally, will have so accustomed the majority of pupils to working with books that they won't give up later. (1988, p.74)

It turns out that every advance is linked to a change in motivations and needs. As students feel encouraged to continue reading, their intellectual potential develops along with their way of critically reading the world. Because critically reading reality means being able to transform it on the basis of what has been known and built up through the pleasure of reading.

The text, when worked on, must provide a leap in quality for the reader's view of the world, both socially and in terms of the reader's daily life, so that reading doesn't lose its validity. The teacher plays a decisive role in mediating the text/reader. In this context, Freire states:

> If the teacher knows the characteristics and dimensions of the act of reading, he or she will be less likely to propose tasks that

<blockquote>trivialize the activity of reading, or that limit the reader's potential to engage his or her intellectual capacities, and will therefore be closer to the goal of training readers. (2005, p.11)</blockquote>

Thus, the search for knowledge can be measured by reading certain texts, but the pedagogical act will require much more than this. Students can pretend that they have read and understood the texts and teachers can pretend that they have believed them, since motivation must come first from the educators. Geraldi observes this situation in the following way: "Teachers, in a historical process that already reveals itself in the birthplace of the university of the school, are today concretely distanced from books and libraries by working conditions and salaries." (1988, p.82)

Therefore, it can also be seen that Brazilian teachers lack reading skills. The excessive number of lessons severely interferes with reading time. In addition, the high cost of books in specific areas is also an aggravating factor that makes it difficult to acquire them.

Therefore, in teaching, it is not enough to discuss or theorize about the value of reading. It is necessary to build and raise the practice so that reading becomes more and more established in the life of the student, because reading is a liberating act. The greater the conscious desire for freedom, the higher the reading rate will have to be.

Achieving these ideals requires a deeper reflection on learning to read, since teaching reading is a continuous process and the teacher, regardless of the subject, is largely responsible for the success or failure of this process.

A teacher who wants to encourage reading must first and foremost be a reader. Only a teacher who is a reader and is aware of the value of reading can create readers and teach them to read the world critically.

1.3. The role of the family

At home or at school, children should have the opportunity to choose the book they want to read, even if they don't get to the end of the story. In this way, it will be possible to form imaginative children with critical awareness and verbal expressiveness. The family environment is the basis for forming a reading habit. For Bamberger:

> Readiness to read is largely determined by the literary and linguistic atmosphere in the child's home [...] before the child is really able to understand the text, parents should read aloud and talk to him about the book [...] in this way, the child's language develops along with his interest in books. Parents need to spend more time with their children, not simply to give them a better standard of living, as is often the case, but to become aware of their children's interests and to be able to take them into account by playing games, reading with them and buying books for them (1988, p.71-73).

In this way, the discovery of the magic of reading takes place at a stage when the bond between parents and children is still very strong. Because of this, the affective is intimately involved in this process. If reading during childhood is associated with moments of pleasure, a positive relationship with books is formed, which is the embryo of an adult reader. Sharing readings is important so that reading is associated with pleasure and not a duty.

According to Sandroni and Machado (1987) the example that children have at home is the most valuable, so when they see their parents "clutching" books, magazines or newspapers on several occasions, they will instinctively value this act.

There are many ways for parents to encourage their children to read:

- Always have books within children's reach. Put a bookcase in your children's room;
- Comment on the books you read as a child or in recent weeks with your children;
- Cultivate the habit of reading at night. Reading aloud in a group can also be enjoyable in a family environment;

- Going to libraries and bookshops;
- Keep books in good condition. That way, children will learn to value them more;
- Giving children pocket money to buy books;
- Ask your children to tell you the story they've read. But at home, never force them to get to the end of a book they don't like. It is therefore appropriate to encourage reading initially, done by parents, because the earlier children are stimulated, the more likely they are to become active readers and citizens.

CHAPTER II

2. LITERATURE: ITS HUMANIZING AND FORMATIVE ASPECT

Literature is essential to the individual and is a precious tool for recovering values such as generosity, solidarity, a sense of justice and collectivity. It develops the capacity for humanization. It organizes emotions and world views; it leads people to reflect on social issues and helps them to take a stand against them. It broadens and diversifies views and interpretations of the world and life.

Thus, literature creates a fictional reality by assuming certain functions that act directly on man and interfere in his formation. Antonio Candido, in A literatura e a formagao do homem (Literature and the Formation of Man) (CANDIDO, 1972) identifies three functions performed by literature, which he calls the humanizing function of literature.

The first of the functions he identified is called the psychological function, because of its strict link to man's ability and need (in the broadest sense of the term) to fantasize. This need is expressed through the daydreams in which everyone is involved on a daily basis, through soap operas, music and fantasizing about love and the future. According to Candido, of these forms of fantasy, literature is the richest.

The fantasies expressed by literature, however, always have their basis in reality, they are never pure. It is through this connection with reality that literature begins to exercise its second function: its formative function.

Literature acts as an instrument of education, of human formation:

> Literature can educate, but not according to official pedagogy. [...]. Far from being an appendage to moral and civic instruction, [...] it acts with the indiscriminate impact of life itself and educates like it. [...] Since literature teaches insofar as it acts with its full range, it is artificial to want it to function like manuals of virtue and good conduct. And society can only choose what it sees fit for its purposes at any given moment, because even the works that are considered indispensable for the formation of the

> world often contain what conventions would like to ban... [...]. It's one of the means by which the young person comes into contact with realities that are intended to be hidden from him (op.cit., p.805).

Through the above quote, we can clearly see the power that literature has to act in the formation of the individual. However, Candido emphasizes that literature can indeed have an educational function, but not to dictate rules to be followed. Literature must educate, it must form, but in a way that is closer to life itself, with ups and downs, ambiguities that lead to the growth and formation of the reader and the human being. Still in Candido's words, "literature neither corrupts nor edifies, but humanizes in a profound sense, because it makes us live". (op. cit., p. 806)

The third and final function, raised by Antonio Candido, concerns the identification of the reader and his or her living universe represented in the literary work. He calls this function the social function. It allows the individual to recognize the reality that surrounds them when transposed into the fictional world, and can cause the reader to integrate into the experiential universe of the characters portrayed, when expressed in a way that is faithful to their reality.

This causes greater integration between reader and character, culminating in the identification of a reality that is not their own, but which is part of their own culture, different from the one in which they participate. This integration makes the reader incorporate the reality of the work into their own personal experiences.

It is clear, then, how important literature is in the social environment, especially for the man who participates in it and is responsible for maintaining it. On the other hand, literature will only fully exercise all its functions when the reader seeks to understand the text, and for this to happen, intense reading practice is necessary.

2.1. A brief history of literature teaching

Analyzing the historical trajectory of the teaching of Literature, we found that this subject has always been linked to the interests of dominant groups and that each era, with its respective philosophy, was taught in a way that could meet certain objectives.

In Greece, literature was synonymous with poetry. From an early age, it took on its educational purpose. Literature's origins lay in myths, from which it inherited its pedagogical character.

As time went by, new genres were added: tragedy, drama and the novel, leading to terminological confusion. Even today it is difficult to define exactly what literature is. According to Magnani (2001, p.6), "According to Vernier, it is best to speak of a literary *corpus*, that is, a set of texts chosen, through value judgments, as literary at a given time and by a given social class".

Until the 18th century, literature was seen as educational. In the Renaissance, it lost its communal character and became private and intimate.

With the emergence of the modern school, learning ceased to be optional and became compulsory; teachers and students were given differentiated *status* and teaching was hierarchized into different grades and levels. From then on, there were continuous assessments to help students move from one stage of knowledge to another.

Firstly, Literature was integrated into the curriculum, dissolving between Grammar, Logic and Rhetoric. Later, it privileged the teaching of classical culture and served as a model for the study of Greek and Latin languages.

From the French Revolution onwards, national literature was introduced into schools by the French and studied from the perspective of literary history. The language of the poets was consecrated as the official language,

The school used literature as a means of disseminating language, culture and national identity, betting on its prestige. As Zilberman (1990 p. 15-16) says: "Literature was institutionalized and ceased to have an intellectual and ethical purpose in order to have a linguistic, vernacular character. (...) These convictions have no pedagogical basis but rather an ideological one, so that confirming them should not be the school's responsibility."

> In Brazil, around the 1970s, vocational education emerged, seeking to use schools to train the workforce for growing industrialization. According to Zilberman and Silva:
> Literature "became a package for quick consumption" in technicist pedagogy. Students only had to read enough to meet the demands of the job market. The summarized handouts, the summaries of novels for the entrance exam, the multiple choice tests corresponded to the ideology of objectivity, total quality and Skinner's behaviorism, on which technicist pedagogy was based. (1990, p.45)

In light of these considerations, we can begin to understand the lack of familiarity with the literary text on the part of students and many teachers. Without reflecting on the fictional, poetic and artistic nature of literature, they end up repeating the information in the textbook.

2.2. Literature at school

According to the National Curriculum Parameters for Secondary Education, Literature should be integrated into Portuguese language reading classes and the teaching methodology should take into account the socio-interactionist nature of verbal language, with the text as the object of work. With regard to the specific nature of literary texts, the PCNs note that: The treatment of oral or written literary texts involves the exercise of recognizing the singularities and properties that nuance a particular type of language use. It is possible to dispel a series of misconceptions that are often present in schools in relation to literary texts, i.e. taking them as a pretext for dealing with other issues (moral values, grammatical topics) than those that contribute to the formation of readers capable of knowing the subtleties, particularities, meanings, breadth and depth of literary constructions. (1998, p.27)

It is well known that the literary text has its own particularities that should be used by teachers as resources to help train their students. However, many educational scholars find fault with the way literary texts are presented in the classroom.

According to Antunes (2003), work with reading is still centered on mechanical skills of decoding writing, often without reflection or dialogue with the text. When reading is used, it serves as a pretext for metalinguistic activities or purely evaluative purposes.

According to Kleiman (2004), there are two conceptions of text and reading that are still perpetuated in schools today. The text is seen as a repository of messages and information and the text is seen as a set of grammatical elements.

Based on these conceptions of the text, the work with reading that derives from them consists of literal copying of expressions from the text, reading aloud, answering interpretation quizzes, extracting the meanings of words. As a result, the artistic nature of the literary text is not respected. As Silva points out:

> Reading for aesthetic pleasure leads to poetry and other literary genres. The horizons offered by literature are unlimited and its interpretations, given the polysemy of the word literary, infinite. The interaction with literary texts, the motivation to search for good authors, greatly nourishes my conscience and allows me to reach the most diverse knowledge. And it is precisely this type of reading that is most damaged in the school environment due to the very distortions that exist in our education system. Instead of pleasure, there is the authoritarianism of compulsory reading, predetermined reading times, reading sheets,

interpretation (as if that were possible!) by the student-reader
and other mechanisms that lead to a dislike of reading and the
gradual death of readers. (1995, p. 55)

Thus, it can be seen that the playful aspects, which should guide children's maturing process through literature, give way to a pedagogical-educational character. In the case of young people, reading becomes an obligation. These factors compromise the formation of the reader, who ends up not seeing books as a source of pleasure. It is therefore up to the school to respect the role of literature as an artistic category, linked to the liberating essence of the human being.

The National Curriculum Parameters for the Portuguese Language (1998, p. 72-73) provide support for schools to work satisfactorily with literature, listing various types of reading that can be carried out with literary texts: "collaborative reading, reading aloud by the teacher, programmed reading and reading of personal choice". However, reading must be carried out in accordance with the textual genre to be used, which in the case of literature means that there are countless possibilities for reading, with different objectives for each type of text.

It is clear that literature should be worked on freely and creatively at school, taking advantage of its permanent dialogue with other arts, to encourage a growing rapprochement between the literary text and the student, as it should be discussed and analyzed by teachers and students, in a relationship of dialogue, exchange and respect for the reader's speech and voice, as well as their previous readings.

2.3 The student / literary text interaction

The literary text has a specific language and proposes an action in the imaginative sphere, creating a new relationship between real situations and situations of thought, thus broadening the field of meanings and helping to form the plans of real life. It deals with the needs of imagination and fantasy, where voluntary rules are created and followed in order to satisfy desire, providing basic structures for changing needs and awareness that lead to advances in the levels of development of the human being.

According to Geraldi (2004, p.91), "reading is a process of interlocution between reader *and* author mediated by the text. (...) The reader is not passive, but an agent who seeks meaning". However, this doesn't always happen, because by not understanding that it is an artistically crafted language and not understanding its vocabulary, the student creates a distance from literature and ends up accepting the teacher's interpretation without promoting a dialogue with the text, thus the text becomes boring and the student is left without stimuli to continue reading.

> Therefore, there is a need for interaction between the student and the literary text so that the reading flows and the student feels motivated to continue with it. Rubem Alves sees the literary text as follows:Every literary text is a musical score. The words are the notes. If the reader is an artist, if he masters the technique, if he surfs over the words, if he is possessed by the text - beauty happens. And the text takes possession of the listener's body. But if the reader doesn't master the technique, if he struggles with the words, if he doesn't glide over them - reading doesn't produce pleasure: we want it to end soon. (2001, correio popular, caderno c)

For Rubem Alves, there are two types of reading: one in which the reader tries to construct meanings for the text; the other is mechanical, carried out only out of obligation, reflecting a lack of knowledge of the nature of the literary text.

However, the clues that the text offers the reader are not all they need to understand a text. Interpreting a text depends to a large extent on knowledge other than language. The reader's knowledge of the world, together with the clues and information provided by the text, form a network of reconstructions of the meaning and intentions intended by the author. For

Silva:

> The subject-reader, based on his or her repertoire of experiences, confronts the literary text in order to construct its meaning and arrive at the referents that demarcate its context [...] Through the text, the author evokes, instigates and indicates referents that the reader also transforms or recreates through a process of attributing meanings." (1995, p.25)

It's clear that the literary text proposes a dialogue with the reader, but for this to happen, the reader needs to enter the text, and to the extent that it arouses the imaginative, the reader draws on their worldly baggage to help them assign meanings to it. It is only through this dialogue that there is interaction between the reader and the text.

In this way, it is worth pointing out that literature can be worked on in such a way as to play its formative and humanizing role. For this to happen, the classroom must be an environment that encourages reading and values the literary text, where it must be contextualized according to each person's reading of the world. Therefore, activities that involve the whole school and community are needed, and these can take the form of projects.

Therefore, the following chapter is intended to present suggestions for teaching projects that have been carried out and have achieved their objectives. To this end, there was a commitment on the part of the professionals involved to carry out quality work based on the teaching and learning of the students. Most of the projects were interdisciplinary, making it easier to achieve the stipulated goals, since the students were able to see that the contents are not isolated, but interconnected, and this association is totally positive for success in teaching.

CHAPTER III

3.   SUGGESTIONS FOR TEACHING PROJECTS

3.1. RECREATING THE LUSIADAS IN COMIC BOOK FORM

3.1.1. Agao

Presenting "The Lusiads" in an attractive way

3.1.2 Title

Recreating "The Lusiads" in comics

3.1.3 **Target audience**: First years of secondary school **CH:**12 h

3.1.4 OBJECTIVE

The project Recreating "The Lusiads" in Comic Books aims to bring students closer to reading, artistic making and the historical and geographical context of the work The Lusiads, demystifying the complexity of literary classics through different approaches and interdisciplinary work, allowing young people to express themselves through a language that is close to their reality.

3.1.5 BACKGROUND

The Lusiadas by Luis Vaz de Camoes deals with the voyages of the Portuguese across "seas never sailed before", one of the characteristics of the epic being the narration of historical or legendary episodes of heroes who possess superior quality. In this way, this teaching project justifies the importance of an interdisciplinary approach, with the support of the Geography teacher. The end result will be adapted to the context of teenagers, since comic books appeal to their popular tastes. The project is in line with the PCNs, as it is clear that through literature, students work on their freedom and creativity, cognition, perception and other aspects linked to their personal growth (PCNs, 2006).

3.1.6 METHODOLOGY

Reading the work. The reading should be done in parts, the student will make notes on what they are reading (bibliographic data binder) as the following steps occur:

a) Historical and geographical context (carried out by the history and geography teacher);

b) Research into mythological elements;

c) Discussion about the students' perception of the work;

Interference in reading is essential for students to be able to understand the work. When the teacher first asks the student to read the entire work and then carry out the other stages, it tends to make the student give up reading, because it is a work that requires more commitment from the reader, due to its complexity.

Afterwards, a lecture on the essential elements of comics;

Creation of comic strips, narrating one of the three major episodes of the novel: Ines de Castro, The Old Man of Restelo and the Giant Adamastor;

Making a mural in the classroom. Details of the activity:

a) Prepare the background for a large mural (in the classroom or schoolyard), preferably in blue, thus recalling the "sea";

b) Organize the students into pairs;

c) Ask them to first make an outline in their notebook of what they want to show;
d) Hand out sheets of A3 paper (A3 paper makes it easier to lay out the drawings);
e) Paste the comics on the mural (in the spaces between the drawings and the blue background, it would be interesting to paste figures of caravels).

Presentation of the groups: Greek Mythology, Spices, Demarcation of the Portuguese Colonies and Religious Conflicts.

3.1.7. GOALS

- Involving students in reading literary texts, specifically "Os Lusiadas";
- Encourage the written production of the comic book genre;
- Promote the interaction of literature with historical, geographical and mythological elements;
- Developing reading and writing skills;
- Developing oral skills through class discussions;
- Promote moments of teamwork;
- Offering students a more playful way of appropriating knowledge;

3.1.8. BIBLIOGRAPHIC REFERENCE

BRASIL, **National Curriculum Parameters** - Part II. Available at: http://portal.mec.gov.br/seb/arquivos/pdf/14 24.pdf. Accessed on 08/ 05/ 2016.http://www.dominiopublico.gov.br/pesquisa/DetalheObraForm.do7select _ action=&co_obra=1870. Accessed on 17/05/2016.
LERNER, Delia. **We need to give meaning to reading**. Nova Escola. Sao Paulo, v 193, p.14, Sept. 2006.
http://guiadoestudante.abril.com.br/estude/literatura/materia_409173.shtml. Accessed on 17/05/2016.

3.1. RELIVING THE CLASSICS

3.1.1. Agao

Bringing the great literary classics into the classroom through an interactive approach.

3.2.2. Title

"Reliving the Classics"

3.2.3. Target audience: high schoolCH: 12h

3.2.4. OBJECTIVE

The main aim of the "Reviving the Classics" project is to encourage students to read the main classics of Brazilian literature, to encourage the habit of reading, to bring students closer to great works and to develop artistic expression.

3.2.5. BACKGROUND

Literary classics need to be given a new focus in order to attract the attention of teenagers. In this way, they need to be involved through a different approach, seeking new strategies for reading the works. Therefore, new approaches are needed, which allow them to expand their creativity, expressing themselves artistically, according to the peculiarities and preferences of each student.

3.2.6. METHODOLOGY

- Reading the realist works: "O cortipo", "O Ateneu", "O primo Basilio", "Memorias Postumas de Bras Cubas" and "Dom Casmurro". (By drawing lots, each group of 5 to 6 students will read one work);

- Historical contextualization in the classroom by the teacher;
- Writing a narrative analysis;
- Choose a day to chat about the books read. Give students a chance to share their desires, difficulties and successes in relation to reading.
- Each group will choose, according to their abilities, a different and creative way of presenting the work, which could include: clips, parodies, drama, plays, choreography, compositions presented with musical instruments, etc;
- Making time available for students in class and student service hours to prepare activities.

3.2.7. GOALS:

- Involving students in reading literary texts, specifically "The Classics";
- Encourage reading;
- Promote the interaction of literature with historical elements and artistic production;
- Developing oral skills through class discussions;
- Promote integration through group work;
- Offering students a more playful way of appropriating knowledge;

3.2.8. BIBLIOGRAPHIC REFERENCE

BRASIL, **National Curriculum Parameters** - Part II. Available at: http: //portal.mec.gov.br/seb/arquivos/pdf/14_24.pdf.Acesso on 08/05/ 2016.
http://www.revistabula.com/647-100-livros-classicos-para-download/. Accessed on 17/05/2016.
http://revistaeducacao.uol.com.br/textos/213/como-estimular-alunos-do-ensino-medio-a-explorar-o-mundo-335642-1.asp. Accessed on 17/05/2016.

3.3. THE TASTE OF CHRONICLES

3.3.1 Apao

Bringing topics that are part of students' daily lives into the classroom is a strategy to encourage them to produce text.

3.3.2 Title

The taste of the Chronicles

3.3.3 Target audience: high schoolCH: 12h

3.3.4 OBJECTIVE

Understand, through the Sabor da Cronica project, language as social interaction and as a symbolic representation of human experiences manifested in ways of feeling, thinking and acting, analyzing, interpreting and applying the expressive resources of languages, relating texts to their contexts.

3.3.5 JUSTIFICATION

The chronicle does not occupy the place that its potential offers. It appears in textbooks broken down into excerpts, as material for language exercises, syntactical analysis or essay topics. In the reading suggested to students, it rarely appears. However, it is a text that is very close to school reality. It starts with its essence, which explores everyday issues and the common man, creating an identification with the student's day-to-day life. Lightness and brevity, the use of simple but well-crafted language and aesthetic sophistication are other points that favor the use of the chronicle in the classroom.

The relevance of this project lies in this list of characteristics, which encourages reading and values it within formal education, thus spreading knowledge about one of the most accessible genres to teachers. The chronicle is multi-faceted, as it deals with politics, family, culture, economics, art, sexuality and cooking, and can be found in letters, magazine articles, books and newspapers. It is light, accessible and has a topical feel, renewing work in the classroom.

In developing this project, students will be encouraged to read, research, compare, debate, create and reformulate ideas. Leaving aside pre-molded and closed schemes, they will broaden their perception of the world, actively participating in an experience of transformation, in a continuous process of construction.

3.3.6 METHODOLOGY

To start the project, we will work on the concept of chronicle, asking each student to research and bring to class a chronicle.

The following topics will be proposed for discussion:

- The chronicle recounts in an artistic and personal way facts from everyday life, usually gleaned from the news. What facts are emphasized in this chronicle?

- A chronicle is usually a short, light-hearted text, written with the aim of entertaining the reader and/or leading them to reflect critically on life and human behavior. How are these two objectives present in the chosen chronicle?

- The narrator in the chronicle can be an observer or a character. How is the narrator of the chronicle analyzed?

- The chronicle generally uses the standard informal variety in short, direct language, close to the reader. Analyze the language used in the chronicle.

To produce the chronicles, students can start from everyday situations. Gathered in small groups, they can identify episodes from everyday school life and comment on them in the form of short chronicles. A total of four texts.

All the chronicles will be checked by another group of classmates, according to the correctness criteria previously established by the teacher. Finally, the texts will be checked by the teacher

At the end, each group will choose a chronicle, which they can either write themselves or research. Three options will be offered, and if any group suggests another activity, it will be analyzed.

The options are:

- Dramatization.
- Comics.

- Multimedia presentation.

To share the work, the teacher should organize an exhibition of the chronicles on the school wall.

3.3.7 GOALS

- Conceptualizing cronica;
- Analyze and identify the chronicle genre;
- Research, read and analyze chronicles, leading students to understand the importance of reading, not only as a way of enriching their vocabulary, but also as a source of cultural wealth;
- Discuss the topics covered;
- Interact with teachers and classmates when researching and writing texts;

- Writing chronicles;

- Recognize and know how to use punctuation to give cohesion and meaning to the text;

- Interpret and criticize results in a concrete situation;

- Find your own way of seeing and questioning the world around you by writing your own chronicle.

3.3.8. BIBLIOGRAPHICAL REFERENCES

BRANDAO, Ignacio de Loyola. **Cronicas para ler na escola**. Rio de Janeiro: Objetiva, 2010.

BRASIL, **Secretaria de Educapao Fundamental: Parametros Curriculares Nacionais: terceiro e quatro ciclos do ensino fundamental: Lingua Portuguesa.** Brasilia: MEC/SEF, 1998.
http://www.madesp.com.br/contaumconto/CRONICAESCREVENDO.HT.
Accessed on 18/05/2013.

3.4. APPLES ARE SIGN OF FALL

3.4.1. Apao

Applying an interdisciplinary teaching methodology to English language teaching.

3.4.2. Title

Apples are sign of fall

3.4.3. **Target audience:** First years of secondary schoolCH : 72 h

3.4.4. OBJECTIVE

Developing an interdisciplinary didactic-pedagogical methodology that discusses the different types of maps, climatic conditions of Brazilian and foreign regions, as well as cultural and nutritional issues involving fruit.

3.4.5. BACKGROUND

In view of the educational scenario, it is necessary to develop activities that are based on the theories of the communicative approach as well as on interdisciplinary work, which prioritizes reading in all its stages, so that the development of reading techniques has real meaning, inserting new technologies as facilitators of learning in the sense of the negotiation of learning and the socialization of knowledge based on Vygotsky's theory.

It can be seen that students finish basic education associating difficulties in understanding text with not knowing the words in the text and that the activity of reading in English is associated with the activity of translation. Faced with this theoretical-practical gap in the process of teaching decontextualized English, it is expected that teachers in higher education take on this commitment, according to Pimenta and Anastasiou (2002).

3.4.6. METHODOLOGY

The English language teacher, together with the plant production teacher on the Agricultural Technician course at the Federal Institute of Technical and Technological Education of Rondonia, Colorado do Oeste Campus, will select the bibliography to be studied by the students on information pertinent to map cultivation involving geographical, economic and cultural aspects, using them as a basic reference.

The participants in the project will be the first year B class, since they had the lowest learning rates according to the statistics for the first two months of 2016. These low rates reveal the need for changes in the context of technical and technological education to meet the new social, political and economic demands brought about by the advance of digital technologies.

By applying teaching strategies permeated by research, students will have the opportunity to become more involved not only with the subject of English, but also with the technical area of plant production. Interdisciplinary work will make a significant contribution to establishing a link between educational practices and the contemporary world of work.

The English teacher will begin the lesson by presenting the vocabulary relating to fruit through dialogued lectures with the support of audiovisual technological resources that enable the development of listening and speaking skills in the English language. It is worth mentioning that this subject of the integrated technical course follows the National Curriculum Guidelines for Secondary Education, in the area of Languages, Codes and their Technologies, which states that "The skills to be developed in the teaching of Foreign Languages in secondary education focus on reading, written practice and contextualized oral communication."

Therefore, when introducing the vocabulary, the teacher should orally use introductory expressions, for example:

Teacher: Today, we are going to talk aboutFruits .
.... fruit).

Today: Our class today is about....fruits. (Our class today is about .... fruits).

The teacher answers one or two examples and these will serve as the basis for the next words, including lessons.

The teacher points to the fruit and introduces it:

Teacher: This is an apple.

Teacher: What is this?

The students answer: Apple.

The teacher emphasizes This is na apple.

Teacher: What color is this apple?

Students may not recognize all the words in the question, but they will recognize the word color, which means color and is cognate. This is a way of encouraging them to use language as a means of communication. Other questions could be asked like. Do you like apple?, What's your favorite fruit? What are the benefits? among others.

After presenting all the vocabulary, the teacher will play a video presenting the vocabulary. It is important that the students listen to it three times. The video will last 4 minutes.

As they watch, ask them if they have any questions. If they don't, the lesson will continue by going back to the slides and asking them to repeat them in English.

At the end of the lesson, the teacher will give the students a handout to practise their writing skills. At the end of each lesson, the teacher will report on the progress of the lesson and put it in the portfolio which will help to analyze the work. The introduction to vocabulary will take two lessons.

The next step will be to divide the class into groups of four students and draw lots of topics to survey the literature on:

- climatic conditions surrounding the production of maps.

- cultural gastronomic characteristics involving the consumption of maps in Brazil.

- cultural gastronomic characteristics involving the consumption of maps and in the United States.

- typical dishes produced in Brazil and the United States with the map.

- nutritional values of the map that contribute to a healthier life.

- eidiomatic curiosities surrounding the map.

After the readings, the students will have two classes to organize the information they consider important for the seminar. The students will have to hand in their notes and comments to the teacher for the portfolio. The Portuguese teacher will be responsible for providing guidance and monitoring the preparation of the fiches.

The English teacher will carry out an experiment with the students which involves planting maps in plastic containers. The instructions will be given in the foreign language. An instructional video will be produced, the main vocabulary of which will be presented to the students beforehand. During the performance, the students will be photographed and the teacher will give the instructions in English. All the students will take part in the experiment. The students must present their experiment on the day stipulated for the seminar presentation, as well as present the fruit growing process at the institution's Technology Week.

In the biology laboratory, the coordinator of the food processing course will carry out an experiment with the students involving the bleaching of maps caused by enzymes. The aim of the partnership is that in addition to the report, which will be guided by the Portuguese language teacher, the students will see the applicability of all the knowledge acquired during the project.

Another option is to visit three supermarkets of different brands to identify the quantity of map-derived products such as cookies, juices, pies, cookies and others. To collect this data, the students will create a table to compare the data. The price, manufacturer, quantity, product and any other characteristics they deem necessary should be taken into account.

The students will have two lessons to write up the information collected in accordance with the institution's academic standards, as well as constructing graphs, banners, posters and videos.

The results will be shared through seminar presentations and tastings of traditional dishes involving maple, the product studied during the two-month period. In addition, the class teacher will contact a state high school and give a lecture on the topic studied throughout the term, as a way of highlighting the importance of studying English as part of technical agricultural education.

3.4.7. GOALS

- To encourage the practice of textual and vocabulary research in the subject of Portuguese Language, facilitating the handling of the textual genres to be used.
- Inserting the use of technological resources in the pedagogical support of English language teaching.

3.4.8. BIBLIOGRAPHIC REFERENCE

BRAZIL. Ministry of Education. Department of Professional and Technological Education. Federal Institute of Rondonia - Colorado do Oeste Campus. Pedagogical Project for the Technical Course in Agriculture Integrated with Secondary Education. Colorado do Oeste, 2012.

FARACO, C. A. e TEZZA, C. **Oficina de texto**. 3. ed. Petropolis: Vozes, 2004.

PIMENTA,Selma Garrido; ANASTASIOU, Lea das Grapas Camargo. **Teaching in higher education**. Sao Paulo: Cortez, 2002.

VYGOTSKY, L. S. **A formagao social da mente**. trad.Grupo de Desenvolvimento e Ritmos Biologicos. Sao Paulo: Livraria Martins Pontes, 1984.

The teaching of reading in English as a second language: some evidence for a grammar centered on the lexicon. Paper presented at the 6th INPLA, PUCSP. INPLA, PUCSP. Sao Paulo, April 26, 1996, p. 106.

http://portal.mec.gov.br/seb/arquivos/pdf/book_volume_01_internet.pdf

http://www.stemilt.com/farm-fork/apples/farming-world-famous-appleshttp://www.stemilt.com/farm-fork/apples/farming-world-famous-apples

http://www.stemilt.com/health-and-nutrition/nutrition/apple-nutrition-

factshttp://www.senept.cefetmg.br/galerias/Anais_2014/GT04/GT_04_x13

x.PDF

3.5. POETIC CLASSIFIEDS

3.5.1. Agao

Work in a playful way so that the student understands the difference between connotative and denotative language.

3.5.2. Title

Poetic Classifieds

3.5.3. Target audience: Junior high school students CH: 12h

3.5.4. OBJECTIVE

Look for strategies so that students understand the difference between connotative and denotative language, observing the uses of the genres studied and the communicative situations.

3.5.5. BACKGROUND

For rent, wanted, needed, exchanged, bought, sold. Verbs in these structures are quite common in classified texts in major newspapers. In order to get to know and practice this type of writing, as well as to differentiate between denotative and connotative languages, this project was conceived.

The name "Classificados poeticos" comes from a book by Roseana Murray, which is used as a reference in the development of this school project. The work promotes the peculiar encounter between the traditional newspaper classified text and the writer's poetic, romantic and playful look at feelings.

3.5.6. METHODOLOGY

Classroom strategies and resources.

1ª Activity:

Organize the class in a circle, find some classified ads and put them in a box. Ask each student to take out an ad and read it aloud to the class. Then ask: What have you just read? Have you seen it somewhere? Do you know the name of this text?

Afterwards, organize the class into groups and present each group with a section of classified ads from a newspaper so that they can observe and understand what kind of ads the newspaper contains, what their characteristics are and how they are organized.

Ask them: What types of ads did you find? Ask this question so that the students can see how the ads are organized into groups: FOR SALE, FOR EXCHANGE, FOR BUY, FOR SALE, among others.

Ask each group to cut out the classified ads according to the specific type. Example:

Ask them to write FOR SALE in their notebooks, then cut out and stick up an advertisement for sale. Then they write BUY IT, cut out and stick a classified ad and so on.

2ª Activity:

Organize the class into four groups. Give each group a statement and a question on the subject. Each color in the example below relates to a group.

ia phrase: Affirmation

2nd sentence: Question

3rd sentence: Likely answer

Then ask the students to record their answers in their Portuguese notebooks, then share and correct them.

3rd Activity:

Tell the students that an author named Rosana Murray has also written some classifieds, but in a different way to the ones that appear in newspapers and magazines. Write the poems on the board and ask them to copy them.

Read the poems with the students and then carry out some activities.

4th Activity:

In pairs, the students will produce poems and then read them to their classmates. The students will choose some poems to display on the school wall.

3.5.7. GOALS

- Identify classified items, recognizing their function;
- Preparing advertisements;
- Reflect on the language of texts;

- Create analogies between texts;
- Create poetic classifieds;
- Bringing students closer to reading in a playful way.

3.5.8. BIBLIOGRAPHIC REFERENCE

BRASIL, Secretaria de Educapao Fundamental: Parametros Curriculares Nacionais: terceiro e quatro ciclos do ensino fundamental: **Lingua Portuguese**. Brasilia: MEC/SEF, 1998.

http://www.anj.org.br/jornaleeducacao/biblioteca/atividades-com-jornal. Accessed on 01/02/2016.

. **Classificados Poeticos**. 1. ed. São Paulo: Companhia Editora National, 2004.

PARANA. State Department of Education. Available at: http://www.portugues.seed.pr.gov.br/modules/galeria/detalhe.php?foto=872&evento= 4. Accessed on September 18, 2013.

PRIETO, Heloisa (Org.). **A Poet's Conversation**. 1. ed. Sao Paulo: Salamandra, 2003. - (Colepao literatura em minha casa; v. 1. Poesia)

SORRENTI, Neusa. **Poetry goes to school: reflections, comments and tips for activities.** Belo Horizonte: Autentica, 2007.

Printed by Books on Demand GmbH, Norderstedt / Germany